"Raising a puppy, the right way"

By

Alexis Robertson

Author: Alexis Robertson

Cover: Alexis Robertson

ISBN: 9789403656588

Puppies are a wonderful addition to any family, but owners can find it a minefield with many questions about how to choose one, how to raise them and how to avoid any behaviours that are seen as socially unacceptable.

I would strongly recommend using the services of an experienced trainer who can help you along your journey.

This book is to help guide you along the way, it covers most of the common questions I am asked frequently by new puppy owners.

I really hope you find this book helpful as my main aim is ensure puppies grow into socially acceptable puppies who get to stay in their forever homes, with you.

I would like to dedicate this book to my assistant trainers who without their support and help at my classes, I wouldn't be able to keep going!!

Bina Martin, Claire Dennis, Sue Archer and Debs Watkins-booth
Thanks ladies, you are my rocks!

But also, to all the clients who have asked for my help with their puppies, followed the training and now have amazing dogs.

And I must mention my cover dogs, Normans, owner Daria.
A prime example of an owner doing everything she can to ensure he grows up to be a social, well-mannered dog.
Read what Daria has to say in my final chapter.

Chapters

Chapter 1

Which breed is right for you?

Choosing to bring a puppy into your home is a massive decision but an amazing one! Dogs are family and will be in your lives for anything up to 20 years and so our commitment to them is extremely important.

What is also important is choosing the right breed.

Firstly, look at your lifestyle, are you active or lazy?!!

How house proud are you, for example, will lots of dog hair or drool be an issue?

Are you prepared to regularly groom your new family member?

Do you want to do an activity with your new dog?

Have you had a dog before or know anything about training good life skills and manners?

Can you afford not just the price of a decent well-bred puppy but also insurance, vets bills and food?

A great way to choose a breed is by making a list of all the things you are looking for in a dog, how much time and energy you wish to give the new puppy and exactly why you want a dog.

Only at that point would I start looking and researching breeds, you see, we are often led by what we think looks cute or is trendy or because we once met a dog that was lovely and so we like the breed.

The looks of a breed are NEVER a reason to get one!

I will give you an example, I love the look of Husky's because I love wolves and they look a bit similar! But I don't have the time or the want to walk/run for miles every day and I don't enjoy grooming dogs! So, clearly, I would not be doing myself or my new puppy any favours if I got one! A good trainer can help you choose and worth contacting one before you start, I have helped several clients.

There is so much information out there on breeds and their character traits and needs, I implore you to research and speak to rescues or breeders who are experienced in the breed you are considering before looking to get one.

Chapter 2

Finding a breeder, the right way

Now you have chosen your breed, the next step is looking for a responsible breeder.
What I mean by this is someone who health tests their dogs before breeding, has a lifetime support package in place and a breeder who finds out all about you before agreeing to home one of their puppies with you!
If a breeder is asking lots of questions and sharing lots of information about their dogs with you, you should be heading along the right lines!

Please ensure you can see the mum, sometimes dad too. Is she friendly and calm or nervous and unfriendly because she may give you an insight into how your puppy may turn out.

Take someone experienced with you, again a dog trainer/behaviourist should know what you need to look out for.

A good place to start is the Assured Breeder's scheme at The Kennel club, these are breeders who have regular checks. You can also check which health tests would be relevant for the breed of your choice.

Sadly, in the UK, there are very limited welfare rules on breeding, and it can be easy to be misled by unscrupulous people.

If you do visit a breeder and it feels wrong or the conditions are not good, please don't buy a puppy, the money will just ensure they continue to abuse the mums and keep breeding.
Instead, contact your local council and the RSPCA, don't let it lie until they visit, after all, every dog's life matters.

Chapter 3

Preparing for puppy to come home

There are lots of things for you to prepare before you collect your puppy.
Some of these are preparing your home, after all, puppies are very intrigued by everything!!

- If you don't want it to get chewed, put it away!
- Decide on your boundaries for your new puppy, where will he/she sleep? Will they be allowed on the furniture/upstairs? (Bear in mind, puppy joints are growing so stairs can be an area where injury can occur)
- Ensure cables are safely tucked away/covered
- Take some time off to allow a settling in period
- Who is going to care for the puppy whilst you are at work? A puppy

may struggle being left for more than an hour or two initially.

- Ensure your garden is secure with decent, secure fencing and a locked gate. With theft on the rise, never leave puppy alone in the garden.
- Whilst talking about gardens, ensure any ponds are puppy safe and check any plants for being poisonous.
- A puppy pen is a great way of keeping puppy safe when you can't watch them but also an ideal place to encourage rest (I will speak more about this later) It allows them to have a safe zone.
- You will need a few bits for puppy too, collar, lead, poo bags, safe chew toys, bowls, and comfy bedding. With regards bedding, don't bother with anything expensive in case you have a chewer! Better to get a single duvet and covers.

The other areas to think about are:

- Choosing a vet, ask for recommendations to find a good one. Register with them once you know when puppy is coming home.
- Insurance, you will probably get a few weeks free from your breeder, but it is well worth researching a lifetime plan that suits you (read the small print!). Vets' bills can be a great expense so if you don't want to get insurance then start a savings pot!
- Find a reputable and experienced groomer, if you have chosen a breed that will require regular grooming/clipping. Ask their advice on what equipment you will need for your dogs' coat.
- Find a reputable trainer who has classes, visit a few and see if you like what is being done. If a trainer refuses to let you watch, walk away! Training classes will be a good idea to start your puppy on their learning journey but only if they are good ones.

Chapter 4

Socialisation, what does it really mean?

When I ask in my classes what the word socialisation means to people, I often get the same answer “meeting other dogs”

Now although this is a small part of socialisation it really isn’t the main factor. In fact, meeting lots of dogs, playing with them etc during puppy hood can lead to big problems in adolescence.
Think about it this way, did you get a dog so that when out on a walk he/she would just go off and play with other dogs? Or did you get a dog to enjoy your walks TOGETHER, as a partnership.
Yes, a puppy needs to see and be around other dogs so that he/she is not afraid of them but do not focus on this aspect of socialisation.

One definition of the word socialisation by the Cambridge dictionary is "the process of training people or animals to behave in a way that others in the group think is suitable"
Puppies will do well to learn to ignore and not be fearful of many objects in the human world that have nothing to do with them.

To fulfil this your puppy needs to learn and have pleasant experiences around everything that we expect them to be able to cope with. The list is quite long but below are some examples:

- Sounds, such as fireworks, thunder, traffic, tv, radio, hoover
- People, including children, elderly, disabled. All people act differently and the more your puppy can see and meet young, the better.
- Other animals, cats, livestock, and small animals. If you have the opportunity, then acquainting your puppy with seeing

these other animals is a good idea. Remember, always do this in a controlled/safe manner.

- Bikes, prams, skateboards, wheelchairs etc. These can be quite intriguing to a puppy, after all, things that move are good for chasing!
- The vet and the surgery, so many dogs are afraid of the vet. This is understandable when often the first few visits involve injections! Ensure you visit the vet's surgery regularly to have pleasant experiences.
- Car travel, they have likely been in a car to get to your home, but this may have been their first time. It is a good idea to lots of small journeys in the car for a few minutes to get your dog more settled.
- Also consider your lifestyle, as an example, if you want them to visit the pub with you think about introducing them to this environment gradually at quiet times.

You will be bringing your puppy home at a vital time in their learning phase, so even if they cannot walk outside due to vaccinations, take them out by carrying them, enabling them to see 'the real world', don't forget, up until now their life has been insular.

The kennel club have a socialisation plan that may be worth a look.

http://www.thepuppyplan.com

Chapter 5

Crate training, or not?

Crates and puppy pens can be extremely helpful during your puppies' younger months.

It can be of benefit to them, a safe place to rest and where you know they are safe when you can't be watching them, but also to your property in terms of keeping furniture from being chewed!

It can also allow for you to keep puppy safe whilst you get them used to you leaving them, this will be covered more in a later chapter.

But a crate/puppy pen is only a safe place if your puppy is comfortable and relaxed inside it.

Some breeders may have already introduced your puppy to a crate, and this can be a great help but if not, you will need to do some work with it to ensure your puppy is happy.

It is important that the dog can stand up, turn around and stretch out, inside the crate. Make the crate comfortable with a bed/blanket inside. You can get a water bowl holder that attaches to the side of the crate to give constant access to water.

Place the crate somewhere that the dog usually lies if possible, or at least in a room where they are comfortable. Keep it out of draughts in winter and away from sunlight in summer. Don't place it in a place where people need to continuously walk past, it should be a place where puppy can rest peacefully.

Stage 1 – Set the crate/pen up and leave the door held open. At mealtimes, place the dog's bowl inside where they need to go in to eat. DO NOT shut the door.

Stage 2 – Once the dog is happy eating and going in and out of the crate, close the door for 1 minute then reopen, stay in the room near the crate.

Stage 3 – Increase the length of time you close the door, giving the dog its meal to occupy, then giving a stuffed Kong, that will last longer.

Stage 4 – Start leaving the room for very brief time during the time the dog is in the crate with door closed. Any whining by the dog should be ignored, returning to the crate when the dog is quiet. Open the door and don't make a big deal about it. Keeping it brief will limit the likely hood of whining. Make sure your puppy has something safe to chew.

Stage 5 – Increase the time you can leave the room, do this at a gradual pace. For example, 1minute to 3 minutes to 10 minutes etc. Only increase the time when the dog seems settled with the previous length of time. Always give the dog interactive food chews and a comfy bed.

Stage 6 – Start going out the house, the first time you should literally walk out the door close it and then return. Increase this in the same way as above.

Once these stages are completed at a pace that the dog can handle, you should build up to maximum of 4 hours. Always leave water, interactive food toys and a comfy bed.

Leave the radio on and for some dogs a piece of clothing that has your scent on it can make them feel more secure.

Take your time, building up your dog's security and emotional state so that it can be left safely, and content takes time. Rushing it will destroy the relationship your dog has with the crate/pen.

Chapter 6

Toilet training

Toilet training is obviously a crucial part of your puppy's early learning. Getting it right is relatively simple but will take a little time and consistency over those first weeks. However, like all things, bad habits learnt early on can lead to problems that may take weeks or even months to resolve.

Personally, I would not use puppy pads, to me this is just teaching them to go inside and so you then must teach them again about the outside!

Initially, you will have to build your daily routine around your puppy's needs. Fortunately, these are quite predictable when they are very young, and with careful supervision you should quickly establish when it is the right time to go outside and minimise any accidents.

Like babies, puppies have poor bladder control, and need to go to the toilet several times an hour when they are awake. They will also usually need to be taken outside first thing in the morning, last thing at night, after each meal, waking from a nap, and after any exercise, play or excitement.

You may find it useful to keep a record of when your puppy sleeps, eats, and goes to the toilet so that you can identify any patterns that emerge. One tip is to use a food timer to remind you when it is time to take your puppy outside to relieve itself. If you find that your puppy needs to "go" every 20 minutes, then set the alarm as soon as he has gone and take him outside the moment the alarm goes off.

Always go with your puppy into the garden and establish a regular spot. Puppies are creatures of habit, so if you introduce the garden to the puppy as its toilet area early on, you should be able to avoid most accidents.

Decide on a cue word or phrase to use when the puppy is going to the toilet, so that the puppy will start to associate the word with the action and should learn to go on command.

By accompanying your puppy into the garden each time, you will be there to attach cue words and praise to any successful actions.

It is likely that there will be accidents. It is important that puppy is not told off AFTER the event, it is only worth saying 'no' if you catch them in the act, and quickly get them outside.

Cleaning the area with an appropriate dog odour remover is very important. A dog's sense of smell is far better than ours and if they can smell urine, it is likely they will 'go' in that spot again!

At night-time, I personally choose to go to bed late and get up early for a few weeks but also sleep in a place where I can hear if puppy wakes up so that I can continue my toilet training by taking puppy straight out and then straight back to bed.

This means that toilet training is 24 hours for a few weeks which makes the process a whole lot quicker!

One common issue I see is when people bring puppies home during the summer months. Often people will say “the door is open, but he still goes inside”

Puppy doesn’t know where we want him/her to go!

If we think about where they were at the breeders, it is usually inside and so puppy has not had the training of where he/she should go.

Following consistent training is the only way puppy can learn where we want them to toilet.

Chapter 7

Setting boundaries and house rules!

Like all of us, puppy needs to learn the house rules and boundaries.

These should be decided before puppy comes home and everyone in the house agrees to stick to them! Such as:

- Should puppy be allowed upstairs.

This is of course up to you but one thing to consider is puppies joints, a puppies joints take at least a year to form and during that time, can easily be injured. For large breeds, consider the damage/dangers of using the stairs.

- Will puppy be allowed on the sofa

This again, is your decision. The same considerations about joints also apply as above. But another consideration is why do they need to be on the sofa so soon! I am not 'anti' dogs being on the furniture, but I would recommend allowing puppy to learn some manners first before giving them so much freedom!

- Where will puppy be when you eat

It may be quite natural for puppy to pester you when eating, this is not a habit to be encouraged and certainly don't feed from your plate or you will regret it!! It could be a good time to give puppy a stuffed Kong or chew in his/her safe place whilst the family eat, especially if you have children.

- What do your children need to know?

Children and dogs can be amazing best friends, but your children need to understand they are not toys and some boundaries are needed.

1. Leave them alone when eating or chewing a bone
2. Let sleeping dog's sleep!
3. Stay out of the crate/puppy pen
4. Touch them gently, no pulling tails/ears etc or hitting.
5. When playing, ensure they have a toy and show them the right way to play

6. Get your children involved in training to help the bond.

Never leave your young children alone with any dogs, even puppies. This is to protect them both.

A houseline can be a great piece of equipment when you have a puppy that you need to manage. The puppy wears it attached to its collar and trails it around, ONLY when the puppy is not alone and never in the crate/pen.

The houseline allows you to remove the puppy or prevent it from doing something without having to touch them. Often when handling a puppy by its collar, particularly if it's being naughty, the puppy will mouth you. This often leads to us letting go and so the dog has learnt one lesson……" use my teeth and I get free!".

This pattern then continues. The houseline saves this from happening and enables you to control puppy appropriately.

Here are some examples of the uses:

Removal from the sofa/bed if you don't want your dog on the furniture.

To take your dog away from trouble.

To have control of your dog when visitors arrive.

To place the dog in a settle if needed.

To use the consequence of Timeout.

Chapter 8

What do you need to know about food and exercise?

Exercise is obviously important for a puppy's wellbeing, but it is very important how much and what type of exercise.

All puppies need at least a year to develop their structure, their bones etc.

Over exercise or chasing balls where twisting and spinning is involved, is very dangerous especially if you have a large breed puppy.

Lead walking on pavements has a harder impact on the dogs' joints so this should be limited, most thoughts are 5 minutes per month. Exercise on soft ground is slightly less harsh and can be included in your walks.

Walks with a puppy at this point should be all about socialisation with sights and sounds, lead training and bonding, not just trying to tire puppy out!

I would strongly advise not to introduce balls and fetch to any puppy until they are in adolescents (over 18 months). To prevent damage to joints but also to prevent an obsession forming with a ball that can end up being their main love in life and ruining future walks where all the dog wants to do is play ball!

When it comes to food it is a bit of a minefield. I am not a nutritionist and so cannot advise you with too many specifics, but I can tell you what I have learned along my learning journey.

What I can tell you is that food plays a major part in their development and can affect behaviour.

Like us, dogs need their nutritional needs met.

For me personally, I like a food such as Butternut Box or raw feeding rather than kibble due to these diets being purer and more natural.

My advice is, do your research. Look at the ingredients and make sure the main ingredient is a real meat, not meat derivatives! Our dogs cannot choose their own food quality, they rely on us to give them everything they need.

Also ensure that you feed them the correct amounts, so many dogs are obese and like us this can shorten their lives.

If at all unsure, seek advice from a canine nutritionist as they are trained to help you. Vets and dog trainers are not necessarily the right people to ask.

Butternut Box

depends on dogs details.

£50.12 +3.99 200g (puppy) 1 pouch
28 pouches for 3 meals.
£65 including postage. adults 300g

wait 2 weeks to change. 7 - 10 days

Bella & Duke

lilys Kitchen

Chapter 9

Don't underestimate the power of rest

Rest is extremely important for puppies. It allows for development.

Believe it or not they need about 20 hours a day!!

Now I often speak to puppy owners who say their puppy never rests during the day, always on the go and struggles to settle. So, they play more with the dog, add enrichment and games into their day to try to settle them.

Unfortunately, this is a big mistake! The puppy that has no rest becomes snappy and irritated.

Instead, what you need to do is 'enforce' rest.

By this I mean following a more structured rest pattern. I'll give you an example.

Play, walk, toilet and training

Followed by popping puppy in a crate or pen with a safe chew and leaving alone for a couple of hours to rest.

Doing this twice a day will help to ensure puppy is not getting overly tired.

With the more active breeds such as border collies and spaniels, people often feel they must keep them active, this really isn't the case. You want them to learn to relax, have an off switch and rest.

Chapter 10

Mouthing and the need to chew!

Puppies love to investigate the world with their mouths!

Teething can also affect the puppy using their teeth all the time on everything and everyone!

The first thing that is important is that you will need to give your puppy plenty of things that he/she can chew, these can range from Kongs, natural chews and nylabones. It is important to note that you should always keep an eye on when toys start to break away and remove them so that the puppy doesn't eat them!

A quick note on what I usually fill Kongs with, I use cooked pasta and cream cheese or a layer around the inside of dog safe peanut butter, you can also use wet dog food.

Many people ask me what to do when puppy starts biting them.

The questions are always, when are they doing this? What are you doing at the time?

Often it is during affection and play.

I always advise you use a toy when playing with your puppy, never rough housing with your hands or encouraging them grabbing your hands.

Affection and play should always stop when puppy starts to use his/her mouth, take your hands away and stop giving attention.

Many puppies can be quite persistent and this needs to be nipped in the bud before they hit adolescence as otherwise mouthing with adult teeth occurs which is not only dangerous if they do it to someone else but also can hurt!

You will often read online that yelping like a puppy will stop them. I have found this rarely works; puppies know we aren't puppies!

It needs to be clear to the puppy that teeth on human skin is not allowed.

I use two ways to deal with this, for some dogs you can clap your hands sharply and say 'no' and the puppy will stop, learning that he/she must not do this.

Another way is 'time out'. For this to work efficiently I use a puppy houseline. The point of the line is to save you having to take the collar of the puppy. Taking the collar just gives them a fantastic opportunity to mouth!

When puppy mouths, you pick up the houseline and remove the puppy from the room for 30 seconds, they must be by themselves. The downstairs toilet or kitchen are good rooms to use. You should never use their crate or puppy pen, as these are their safe areas.

Rest also plays a part in the mouthing, the more over tired your puppy is the more irritable they become and therefore more mouthing!

When it comes to chewing furniture and such, it really is dependent on the individual dog. Some are much more into this than others!

To try to limit this, think carefully where you leave puppy when not supervised. Refer to the crate/puppy pen training in a previous chapter. Making sure your puppy has plenty of safe chew toys.

And one important lesson that puppies teach us……. Put things away!

If you don't want shoes etc chewed up, get used to putting things away to keep them safe whilst puppy grows and learns.

Chapter 11

Jumping up, how to stop reinforcing it

A common issue that people call me about is jumping up.

There is a reason dogs jump up to greet us, it's because if you watch 2 dogs who know each other greet each other, they will nuzzle/lick faces. I always think that dogs jump at us to greet in the same way, it's just our faces are so high up!

You may not even mind your puppy jumping at you, but you need to think about what your dog is learning and what they will do when greeting strangers out and about.

Just think about this for a moment, your adult dog is off lead in a park and sees a person walking. Being friendly your dog runs over and jumps up to say 'hi', the person is knocked over and hurt. Now if they really want to, they are within their rights to speak to the authorities and now you find yourself in trouble.

This may seem dramatic, but it is reality!

You must think about what you are teaching your puppy when you come home and greet them.

If you allow or worse still encourage them to jump up at you, you are teaching your puppy that when greeting people, they will get praised and affection for jumping.

One of the best things you can do is teach them as early as possible that jumping up gets no attention.

Follow the simple rules to help achieve this from the minute you bring puppy home:

- Do not touch your puppy if jumping
- Do not speak to your puppy if jumping
- Do not look at your puppy if jumping
- When you reunite with your puppy at any time, keep calm and ignore him/her

until they calm down and keep all 4 paws on the floor.

Sticking to these simple rules from the minute puppy comes home can teach them not to jump as it has no value to them.

Don't think to yourself that it won't be an issue and puppy will grow out of it because they won't! Best to never teach them that jumping up is rewarding in the first place.

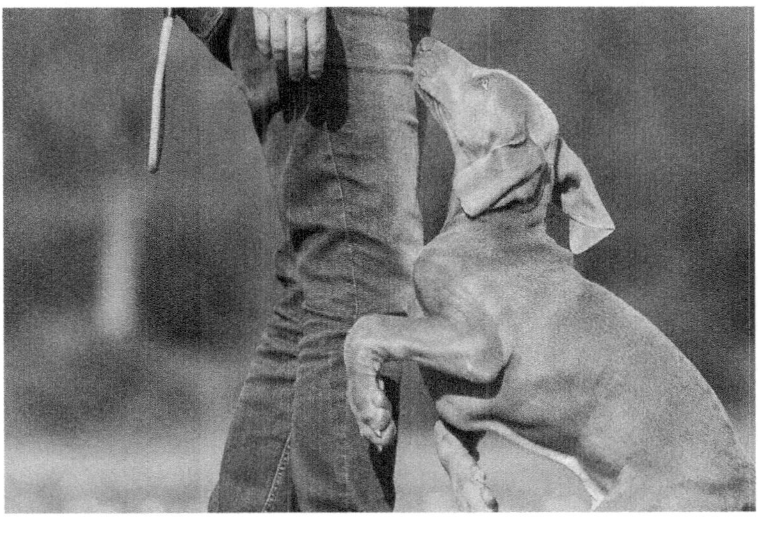

Chapter 12

Learning to be home alone

Every dog needs to be left home alone at some point and this can seem very daunting and stressful to a dog who doesn't learn to feel safe and getting used to it early on can help.

I find it best to leave them in their crate/pen or room by themselves whilst you are still in the house first can help with you leaving the home.

Make sure puppy has had some activity, relieved itself and has something to chew on. I always leave a radio on as well to drown out the outside noises.

It is very easy for puppies to become too reliant on us because we allow them to demand attention all the time, following us around! It is important to not allow this to go on otherwise they really can't cope when we leave the house!

Combining the leaving them with the rest periods mentioned in the previous chapters can really help them learn independence.

You can play a part in how they feel when you leave by not making a big deal of it! Try to ignore puppy for 5-10 minutes before you go and the same when you return, doing this helps with independence and when we make a deal out of it, it is easy for us to make them feel worried!

It can be helpful to leave them a piece of your clothing that has your scent on it, a chew item that is safe to be left with always make sure they have been to the toilet.

Leave your puppy regularly for short periods at first to make it seem like the norm. Never go back to them when there is any crying or barking, wait for 30 seconds of silence before entering the room where puppy is.

The indoor cameras that are available nowadays can be very useful tools to keep an eye on your puppy when you leave them.

Chapter 13

Barking, what can it mean?

Once puppy finds his/her voice there are several areas that may become a nuisance if left!

One of these is alert barking at the door etc.

Alert barking is perfectly normal and most of us like it that our dogs behave like that, to warn off baddies!

But it is more an issue if your puppy can't stop, and the barking becomes excessive which can lead to it being a nuisance to neighbours.

When puppy starts to bark at the door, say 'quiet' firmly but not shouting. If puppy stops, reward with several small treats and say, 'good quiet'. If puppy doesn't stop, take them by the collar or a puppy houseline and time them out in another room (downstairs toilet or kitchen are ideal) for 30 seconds alone. Open the door after the 30 seconds ONLY if they have stopped barking.

Attention seeking barking is the other most common reason puppies' bark.

It is easy to spot this one as the puppy will usually be looking at you as they bark.

For this one you can do the time out mentioned above or the opposite, which is to walk away from the puppy yourself and leave the room.

Attention barking will cease if the puppy doesn't get the attention, he/she wanted.

Giving attention means looking, talking, or touching your puppy.

Chapter 14

Do you need to train puppy?

Today our dogs are under a lot of pressure to be well behaved and socially acceptable and yet our lives are so much busier and stressful.

Our dogs need and deserve to be shown how we would like them to behave, to help them become confident and social.

Certainly, for most puppies, getting into classes early is ideal, the trainer's job is to help you train your puppy.

But it is so important that you go to the right kind of classes. Check out the trainer, look for recommendations and if you can, go and watch a class.

Bad training can be worse than no training!

With regards socialisation or puppy parties, these are very hard to find good ones! A free for all of puppies running around play fighting, can be a recipe for disaster. It teaches some puppies to bully and can also terrify less confident puppies.

They are also often run by vet practices or pet shops, it's just my opinion but these people haven't necessarily trained in dog behaviour and may not know what they are looking for when it comes to the wrong type of behaviour, that could be detrimental to your puppy.

Puppies need to learn to bond with you, so there is no need for off lead social play with other dogs at this point.

Much better to go to a training class where you will learn how to help your puppy develop and grow into a socially acceptable dog.

To find a trainer in your area, check out the PDTI website.

www.pdti.org

If you're in Kent, check out my website

www.kentcompaniondogtraining.co.uk

Chapter 15

Norman's story

When I was getting ready to bring my puppy home, I knew I would take him to puppy class so he could become a well-socialised, easy-going dog. However, when Norman finally arrived, it surprised me how crazy puppies can get. Quickly I realised I might need some help before he gets his second round of jabs and can go out to attend the class. So, I researched and contacted Alexis to book our first 1:1 session. Norman is a double doodle and would become a big dog, so I wanted to ensure I could control him to keep him safe and make our life together pleasant.

The first meeting changed my view on dogs. I was surprised by my wrong impression of the purpose of walking and playing and how little I knew about the power of mental stimulation. However, it helped me understand Norman's needs and behaviour better. After the session, I was determined to do all my homework, especially since I saw how quickly my puppy was responding to training, and I knew if I put effort into it, I could raise a well-behaved dog. So, I followed Alexis' advice about walks, basic training, and playtime, and after a few days, I could see a significant change in my dog's behaviour. His naps were longer, his excitement was more contained, and he bit less.

Norman gained a lot from this experience. But he wasn't the only one who benefited from it. After each session, I felt good about myself as a confident dog owner. I learned a lot, and training Norman stopped being a chore. It became my hobby. I even decided to expand my knowledge and joined an instructor course.

I might make it sound effortless, but it wasn't all the time. There were times when I would cry because of frustration when Norman peed on a floor for the 15th time. Or when I went to the toilet to come back to a chewed-up stolen item. However, I could always text Alexis, and she always came up with a new approach to the subject. So, this again emphasises how important it is to have a good trainer on board. After a few months, I learned consistency is the key. But also, you need to be very patient and relaxed. And there will always be worse days, but it's ok to let go and just play with your puppy. There is always tomorrow to resume training.

If I can give a piece of advice, it would be 'don't have set training sessions, just look for opportunities. So, for example, I practise with Norman when my tea is brewing, when my son is getting ready to go to school or when I need a break from work and take my eyes off a monitor.

If I could change one thing in my and Norman's journey, I would have asked Alexis to come and help me before I brought him home. Then, she would be able to save me a lot of stress by pointing out which parts of my house could be puppy-proofed better, what type of food and treats are the best, and what I can expect in general as a first-time puppy owner.

So, everybody who is considering getting a dog - do it! It's a beautiful thing to live with such a loyal and loving companion. But before you do, find an experienced trainer, and discuss your lifestyle, expectations, and budget so they can help you find the perfect match.

Written by Daria

Gallery of some of my puppy clients

It has been a pleasure working with all these beauties

Useful links

www.kentcompaniondogtraining.co.uk

If you are in Kent, contact me if you need any 1:1 help or would like to join my classes.

www.pdti.org

To find a trainer in your area

www.thekennelclub.org.uk

To look at the Assured Breeders scheme list of breeders. You can also find all the info you will need about health testing.

www.butternutbox.com/KentCompanion

Using my link will get you a large discount with this great nutritional food.

www.bybenji.com

These treats are great for training, with no artificial ingredients.

Printed in Great Britain
by Amazon

26665640R00040